FIND FREEDOM

Billy Graham

FIND
FREEDOM

ZONDERVAN
PUBLISHING HOUSE
OF THE ZONDERVAN CORPORATION
GRAND RAPIDS, MICHIGAN 49506

FIND FREEDOM
Formerly published as
FREEDOM FROM THE SEVEN DEADLY SINS
Copyright 1955 by
The Billy Graham Evangelistic Association
1620 Harmon Place, Minneapolis, Minnesota

Library of Congress Catalog Card Number: 72-81048

Twenty-second printing   1977
ISBN 0-310-25062-5

Printed in the United States of America

INTRODUCTION

After a minister had spoken strongly against sin one morning, one of his members said, "We don't want you to talk so plainly about sin because if our boys and girls hear you mention it, they will more easily become sinners. Call it a mistake if you will, but do not speak so bluntly about sin."

The minister went to the medicine shelf and brought back a bottle of strychnine marked POISON. He said, "I see what you want me to do. You want me to change the label. Suppose I take off this 'poison' label and put on some mild label such as 'peppermint candy.' Can't you see the danger? The milder you make the label, the more deadly the poison."

During the last few years we have been putting a mild label on sin. We've called it "error," "negative action" and "inherent fault." But it is high time that we put a POISON label back on the poison bottle and not be afraid to be as plain as the Bible is about the tragic consequences of sin.

Pope Gregory the Great, at the end of the

sixth century, divided all sins under seven heads. He said that every sin that a man commits can be classified by seven words. He named the sins: pride, anger, envy, impurity, gluttony, slothfulness and avarice. They have been called down through the centuries "the seven deadly sins." These sins are nowhere collectively mentioned in a single passage in the Bible, and yet they are all condemned separately in many places. Thomas Aquinas and most of the great theologians have agreed with Pope Gregory, and these seven deadly sins have become a recognized part of moral theology.

These sins also became the subjects of poets. The scheme of Dante's "Purgatory" follows the order of the seven deadly sins. They are also discussed fully in Chaucer's "Parson's Tale" and in Marlowe's "Doctor Faustus." Even a recent Italian movie was entitled "The Seven Deadly Sins."

The following messages, with very little editing, are just as they were given on seven consecutive broadcasts of "The Hour of Decision."

CONTENTS

Introduction

FIND FREEDOM

1

PRIDE

The first of the seven deadly sins is pride. It naturally comes first — for as we read in Proverbs 16:18, "Pride goeth . . . before a fall." Pride is thus the mental and moral condition that precedes almost all other sins. All sin is selfishness in some form or other, and pride consists essentially in undue self-esteem, delighting in the thought of one's own superiority over his fellows. The Scripture says in Proverbs 16:5, "Everyone that is proud in heart is an abomination to the Lord: though hand join in hand, he shall not be unpunished." Again in Proverbs 29:23 we read, "A man's pride shall bring him low: but honor shall uphold the humble in spirit."

The pride that God loathes is not self-respect

or a legitimate sense of personal dignity. It is a haughty, undue self-esteem out of all proportion to our actual worth. It is that repugnant egotism which is repulsive to both man and God. It is that revolting conceit which swaggers before men and struts in the presence of the Almighty. God hates it. It is an abomination unto Him, which means that it makes Him shudder. God has said in Psalm 101:5, "Him that hath a high look and a proud heart will not I suffer." God cannot stand or endure pride. He hates it!

Pride may take various forms, but it all emanates from the haughty human heart. Some take pride in their looks, others in their race, others in their business, others in their social life. In other words, pride may be spiritual, intellectual, material or social. The most repugnant of these four is spiritual pride. This pride of the spirit was the sin that caused Lucifer, the Devil, to fall. This is where sin actually began.

We read in Isaiah 14:12-15, "How art thou fallen from heaven, O Lucifer, son of the morning! how art thou cut down to the ground, which didst weaken the nations!

"For thou hast said in thine heart, I will ascend into heaven, I will exalt my throne above the stars of God: I will sit also upon the mount of the congregation, in the sides of the north:

"I will ascend above the heights of the clouds; I will be like the most High.

"Yet thou shalt be brought down to hell, to the sides of the pit."

Here we find Lucifer saying, "I will," five times. "I will be above God." It was the pride of his heart that was the first sin ever committed in the universe. When we, like Lucifer, begin to feel that we are self-contained and self-sufficient, we are on dangerous ground.

Spiritual pride, because it trusts in one's own virtue rather than the grace of God, is earmarked for God's judgment. It induces in us a contempt for others, and makes us contemptible to those about us. It says with the repulsive Pharisee of old, "God, I thank Thee that I am not as other men are." It is smug, self-satisfied and full of conceit. God loathes spiritual pride because it presumes to be good in its own right. It is the strutting of a tramp clad in filthy rags who imagines that he is the best dressed of all men. Spiritual pride would be humorous if it wasn't so tragic. God has sounded a stern warning for these descendants of the Pharisees. He has said in James 4:6, "God resisteth the proud, but giveth grace unto the humble."

There are some people who think they have a corner on the Gospel. They have become conceited, smug, proud and pharisaical. There are others that glory in their self-righteousness, and think that they are better than other people. They don't do this, and they don't do that. They keep the letter of the law, but have long since forgotten the spirit of the law. They are guilty of spiritual pride. There are also others who think themselves to be pure and all others impure. They have forgotten that there is no such thing as a completely pure church. Jesus taught that the chaff and the wheat would grow together and that we would not be able to distinguish them until the end of time. Yet

we have many Pharisees today going about trying to throw the chaff out of the wheat, doing
that which God said could never be done until
Christ comes again. We have many going about
pulling specks out of other people's eyes when
they have beams in their own eyes. They have
a haughty, superior, "chip on the shoulder" attitude. They spend their time criticizing and
gossiping about others. This is the worst pride
of all.

Another form of pride is intellectual pride.
The Bible says to those who suffer from this kind
of spiritual delusion in I Corinthians 8:1, 2, ". . .
Knowledge puffeth up, but love edifieth. And
if any man think that he knoweth anything,
he knoweth nothing yet as he ought to know."
This kind of pride manifests itself in arrogance
toward the unlearned, the illiterate and the oppressed. It forgets that our mental capacities
were given by God, and that the knowledge
we attain is largely the labor of others. Is this
a reason for intellectual arrogance? Paul says
in Romans 12:16, ". . . Mind not high things,
but condescend to men of low estate . . ."

The philosopher Plato once entertained some friends in a room where there was a richly ornamented couch. One of his friends came in, very dirty as usual, and getting on the couch and trampling on it said, "I trample upon the pride of Plato." Plato mildly answered, "But with greater pride, my friend."

Intellectual pride is too often the enemy of the Gospel of Christ because it gives its possessor self-confidence rather than God-confidence. We read in Proverbs 3:5, "Trust in the Lord with all thine heart; and lean not unto thine own understanding." But the intellectually proud are not like that. They like to put God in a test tube; and if He cannot be put in a test tube, then they cannot accept Him. They do not like to lean on Him and trust Him. They cannot understand that faith goes beyond learning, knowledge and even reason, and accepts that which may not even appear logical to the mind. To have knowledge without faith is to use only half of your mind. The Psalmist says in Psalm 111:10, "The fear of the Lord is the beginning of wisdom . . ."

True religion, contrary to the conception of some, increases your intellect rather than distracts from it. Paul, himself an intellectual, said in Romans 12:2, ". . . be ye transformed by the renewing of your mind . . ." The kind of intellectual pride that is given to intolerance, bigotry and smugness, God hates. God abhors intellectual pride. He says in Proverbs 26:12, "Seest thou a man wise in his own conceit? there is more hope of a fool than of him."

Still another manifestation of pride is the pride of material things. Material possessions, like other blessings, flow from God. The Lord says in Deuteronomy 8:18, "But thou shalt remember the Lord thy God: for it is He that giveth thee power to get wealth . . ." In I Chronicles 29:12 David says, "Both riches and honour come of Thee, and Thou reignest over all; and in Thine hand is power and might, and in Thine hand it is to make great, and to give strength unto all."

In material pride, self is enthroned instead of God. Secondary things are exalted to a place of first importance, and life gets out of balance.

The individual then begins to concentrate on what he has rather than on what he is in the sight of God, and the soul begins to shrivel. Material pride tends to make a man covetous. The lust for money can be more habit forming than the thirst for drink. We are warned in Psalm 62:10, "Trust not in oppression, and become not vain in robbery: if riches increase, set not your heart upon them." The Bible again warns in I Timothy 6:9, "They that will be rich fall into temptation and a snare, and into many foolish and hurtful lusts, which drown men in destruction and perdition."

All the material things that you have come from God. The ability to accumulate wealth comes from God. The time you are allotted to enjoy material things comes from God. So why all this unjustified human pride of your possessions? James 1:17 teaches that "Every good gift and every perfect gift is from above . . ." You have absolutely nothing that you did not receive from God. He gave you the strength to work, a mind to think and a great country

like America where you have had freedom of
opportunity. It all came from God.

Then there is social pride. This manifests
itself in class, racial and caste arrogance. A
world statesman has said that the tiny atom
made us all the same size. God does not make
the distinctions in men that men make between
themselves.

There are few people today who really believe in the super race. The idea of a super
race is unBiblical, unScriptural and unChristian.
While touring Germany I heard a great deal
about Hitler who believed in a super race. His
view upset the world and devastated a great
nation.

How many people have social pride that is
sinful? It is interesting to note on great state
occasions that the ambassadors and rulers of
small nations are resplendent in gold braid and
glittering apparel, but the representatives of
the great nations are distinguished by their
modest attire. A zebra is more gaudy than
a workhorse, but the lowly horse is loved most
because he serves us best.

Yes, the Bible teaches that pride is sin. Any kind of pride is a stumbling block to the kingdom of God. The greatest sin that will keep men and women from the kingdom of God is the sin of pride. Pride is the sin that God seemingly hates most.

What can you do about it? Confess your pride. Humble yourself in the sight of God. Come to the Cross of Jesus Christ, and "Let this mind be in you, which was also in Christ Jesus" (Philippians 2:5). No man will ever get to the Kingdom proudly. No man can walk up to God with pride in his heart and be received. You can only come to God when you humble yourself, acknowledge your sin and receive Jesus Christ as your Saviour.

2

ANGER

Anger is one of man's most devastating sins. This is one sin which everyone is capable of committing. The tiny baby has a fit of temper and loses its dinner. The little boy has a tantrum and upsets the family decorum. The wife loses her temper and develops a sick headache. The husband gets angry and loses his appetite. Every member of the family is subject to its blight. No one is by nature immune to this dispositional disease of human nature.

Anger breeds remorse in the heart, discord in the home, bitterness in the community and confusion in the state. Homes are often destroyed by the swirling tornadoes of heated domestic anger. Business relations are often shattered by fits of violent temper when reason gives way to venomous wrath. Friendships are often broken by the keen knife of indignation, which is sharpened by the whetstone of anger.

Anger is denounced by the church and condemned by the sacred Scriptures. It murders, assaults and attacks — causing physical and mental harm to its victims. Its recoil, like a high-powered rifle, often hits back at the one who wields it, doing equal damage to the offender and the offended.

Because anger has brought so much unhappiness and confusion to the world, God loathes it. In Psalm 37:8 we read, "Cease from anger, and forsake wrath; fret not thyself in any wise to do evil." Jesus condemned it in no uncertain terms and classed it with the heinous sin of murder. He said in Matthew 5:22, "I say unto you, That whosoever is angry with his brother without a cause shall be in danger of the judgment: and whosoever shall say . . . Thou fool, shall be in danger of hell fire." The wise Solomon said in Proverbs 16:32, "He that is slow to anger is better than the mighty; and he that ruleth his spirit than he that taketh a city." The Bible again says in James 1:19, "Wherefore, my beloved brethren, let every man be swift to hear, slow to speak, slow to anger."

Anger is a heinous sin because it reveals the animal nature of man. Many people are charming, lovable and likeable until they become obsessed with a fit of rage, and then they are transformed into repulsive, irrational creatures more like wild beasts than civilized men. Doctors tell us that when any human emotion is overstimulated, excessive amounts of adrenal are supplied by nature to replenish the emotional drain on our systems. The person with a violent temper uses up this extra supply of energy to feed the flame of his passion rather than to put out the fire.

Anger not only brings out the animal nature of man, but hinders Christian testimony. Peter, angered at the Roman soldiers, grabbed a sword and cut off the servant's ear; but Jesus reproved him for his angry spirit and said in Matthew 26:52, ". . . they that take the sword shall perish with the sword." Many a Christian witness has been ruined by carnal anger.

A professed Christian woman was very anxious for her husband to find Christ. One day her minister spoke to her husband about his soul, and the minister was taken aback when the man said, "I'm not particularly an irreligious man, but if Christianity should make me wrathy like my wife, I want no part of it."

The minister went to the lady in question and told her precisely what her husband had said. She had not realized that her temper had been so out of control, and she was repentant about it. Together the minister and the woman knelt in prayer while she sobbed her heart out to God.

A few days later the husband had been out fishing; and when he came into the house with his rod over his shoulder, he accidentally hit a costly lamp which went crashing to the floor. He stood with his hands over his ears waiting for the second crash of his wife's anger—but it never came. He looked up to see his wife smiling as she said, "Don't worry about it, dear. Accidents happen in the best of families."

"You mean you're not angry as usual?" he asked.

"No, dear, that's all a thing of the past. I'm sorry I've been so impatient, but God is helping me to gain control of my temper."

A few Sundays later the husband joined the church. Her testimony had been strengthened by her anger being controlled by the Spirit of God.

Anger also causes people to lose the joy of living. In Genesis 4:6 God said to Cain, whose joy had been expelled by anger, ". . . Why art thou wroth? and why is thy countenance fallen?" The bad thing about losing your temper is that other things are often lost with it. When temper rages, your good expression goes. When temper rages, your reputation goes. When temper rages, your friends go. When temper rages, your opportunity goes. When temper rages, your testimony goes.

Anger is the parent of murder. Cain was wroth before he murdered Abel. It cocks the

assassin's pistol, dispenses the killer's poison and
sharpens the murderer's dagger. It devastates,
mutilates and destroys. It kindles the fire of
passion, fans the flame of envy and leaves the
soul barren and desolate. Here, of course, we
are speaking of irrational, unjustifiable anger—
the kind that goads the conscience, lashes out
at the innocent and induces malice and discord
in the home and in society. This kind of anger
God hates.

Too many of us are guilty of this blighting
sin. Though we excuse ourselves by blaming
our uncontrolled anger upon our natural dispo-
sition, down deep inside our conscience tells us
that it is wrong. There is the haunting con-
viction that we are grieving the Spirit of God
when we are ruled by violent temper.

What can be done about this dispositional
sin? Does the Christian faith have an answer?
Can Christ calm the tempestuous sea of anger as
He did the turbulent Sea of Galilee long ago?
If there were no way to overcome anger, if
there were no way to bring it under control,
God would never have said in Psalm 37:8,

"Cease from anger and forsake wrath." God never demands an action which is impossible of achievement. There is a victory—in Christ— over sinful anger. Even Plutarch said, "I have learned that anger is not incurable if one wants to cure it."

The first step then in finding victory over unjustified anger is to want to get rid of it. The will comes to the fore and says, "I will do something about this unruly temper of mine." This means that you stop justifying yourself by saying, "My whole family is quick-tempered—I inherited it from my mother." Or, "Everyone loses his temper some time or other—what's wrong with that?" You must recognize it as an ugly, venomous sin both in the eyes of God and in your own sight.

Secondly, we must confess this evil anger to God and ask His forgiveness for fits of rage and uncontrolled temper. If anger is a sin and if being angry with one's brother without a cause brings the judgment of God, we ought to hate it, despise it and seek by divine methods to overcome it. In I John 1:9 we read, "If we confess our sins, He is faithful and just to forgive us our sins, and to cleanse us from all unrighteousness."

Anyone knows that hot, violent anger is unrighteous and unChristlike. God, in love and mercy, has promised both to forgive us of the sin of anger and to cleanse us from it. This does not imply that people become spineless, bland creatures without any spunk or spirit, but it does mean that our tempers which were used in wrath now become things of blessing. The tongue which once was used for profanity now becomes an instrument of praise. The hands which once hurt now become healing hands. The feet which once walked the pathways of violence now walk the pathways of love and service. The wild horses of passion are tamed by the Spirit and become our servants rather than our masters. That is exactly what Jesus meant when He said, "Blessed are the meek."

Remember Peter—before the resurrection and the descent of the Holy Spirit? He swore in the camp of the enemy, denying his Lord, and became enraged at the soldiers who took Jesus into custody. His angry spirit was a poor witness for a disciple of the lowly Galilean. But after the Spirit of God came into his heart on the day of Pentecost, his temper was brought under control. Never again was his tongue employed in profanity. Never again were his hands used in violence. Never again was his voice raised in denial of his Lord. Never again were his feet found in the camp of the enemy. Peter's temper was not gone—it had been diverted to a constructive purpose. It had been bridled by the Spirit of God. Conversion to Christ had not made him weaker—it had made him a stronger man. No longer was he sinfully angry.

You can become a meek man. The word "meek" actually means that you become controlled by the Spirit of God. As a wild force tamed, so the Spirit of God can tame your tongue and tame the passions of your soul, if you surrender your heart and your life to Jesus Christ.

However, we are taught in the Bible that there is a righteous indignation that is legitimate and justified. In fact, if we do not have righteous indignation on occasion, we may actually be sinning. So there is a type of anger that is justified and commended in the sight of God.

Now that type of anger is this. We are to be angry—we are to have righteous indignation at sin and corruption and immorality round about us. We are to have righteous indignation at the filthy literature that is on our news stands. We are to have righteous indignation at some of the evil corruption in high places that is uncovered from time to time. We are to have righteous indignation about the corruption in many of our cities and the gangsters who walk our streets. We are to have righteous indignation against these things.

There is a third kind of anger and that is the anger of God. In Romans 1:18 we read, "For the wrath of God is revealed from heaven against all ungodliness and unrighteousness of men who hold the truth in unrighteousness." Again we read in Colossians 3:6, "For which things' sake the wrath of God cometh on the children of disobedience." God is a holy and a righteous God and His eyes are too pure to look upon evil. When sin is in His sight, God's holiness explodes into wrath and anger against sin.

Men and women who have not come to the Cross of Christ, who have not come to acknowledge their sin and receive Him as Saviour, are in for the wrath of God. There is a day of judgment coming when the holy wrath and anger of God will be exploded against the sinner who has not received His Son, Jesus Christ, as Saviour. If you have not received Christ—at the day of judgment when you come before Him, He will say, "Depart from me, ye cursed, into everlasting fire prepared for the devil and his angels" (Matthew 25:41).

3

ENVY

Envy and jealousy can ruin reputations, split churches and cause murders. Envy can shrink our circle of friends, ruin our business and dwarf our souls. Procrastination may be the thief of time, but envy is the murderer of souls. We read in Job 5:2 that it can kill a person (modern psychiatry bears this out), "For wrath killeth the foolish man, and envy slayeth the silly one."

There is a Greek story about a man who killed himself through envy. His fellow citizens had erected a statue to one of their number who was a celebrated champion in the public games. But this man, a rival of the honored athlete, was so envious that he vowed that he would destroy that statue. Every night he went out into the darkness and chiseled at its base in an effort to undermine its foundation and make it fall. At last he succeeded. It did fall—but it fell on him. He fell, a victim of his own envy.

The Bible, whose counsel is wiser than top psychiatrists, tells us not to be envious of the rich. In Psalm 49:16 we read, "Be not thou afraid when one is made rich, when the glory of his house is increased." Envying those who are more prosperous than we are does not add one dollar to our assets, but it bankrupts the soul. The envious man somehow feels that other people's fortune is his misfortune, that their success is his failure and that their blessing is his curse. The irony of it all is that if he builds up such a case in his mind and soul, his failure is inevitable. I have never seen a man who profited in any way by being envious of others, but I have seen hundreds cursed by it.

You cannot have a full orbed personality and harbor envy in your heart. We are told in Proverbs 14:30, "A sound heart is the life of the flesh, but envy the rottenness of the bones." Envy is not a defensive weapon—it is an offensive instrument used in spiritual ambush. It wounds for the sake of wounding and hurts for the sake of hurting.

"Tell me," said the willow to the thorn, "why art thou so envious of the clothes of those who pass by? Of what use can they be to thee?"

"None whatsoever," replied the thorn. "I have no desire to wear them—I only want to tear them."

How like that thorn is the envious person— reaching out to destroy others without bringing any profit to himself.

Envy is one of the most heinous sins of the flesh and one of the most uncalled for. It is strongly denounced by the wise men of the ages and certainly denounced by God.

Solomon said in Proverbs 27:4, "Who is able to stand before envy?"

In Galatians 5:26 Paul said, "Let us not be desirous of vain glory, provoking one another, envying one another."

James said, "Where envying and strife is, there is confusion and every evil work" (James 3:16).

Francis Bacon said, "Neither can he that mindeth his own business find much matter for envy. For envy is a gadding passion, it walketh the streets and doth not stay at home."

Horace said, "Than envy, Sicilians have invented no worse torture."

Horace also said, "The envious man grows thin at another man's prosperity."

Samuel Johnson said, "Envy is the only passion which can never lie quiet for want of irritation."

Petronius said, "The vulture who explores our inmost liver and drags out our heart and nerves is not the bird of whom our poets talk, but those diseases of the soul—envy and wantonness."

Envy, according to the Bible, is inherent in our very nature. We read in James 4:5, "The spirit that dwelleth in us, lusteth to envy." Cain envied Abel because he had found favor with God—and then murdered him. Envy needs no justification to make an attack. More often than not, there is no real reason for its existence. It springs from the unregenerate human heart as naturally as weeds grow in a flower garden.

Joseph's brethren were envious of him and

sold him into Egyptian slavery. They paid for their deed with a perilous famine, and in the end were forced of necessity to recognize Joseph's superiority. Their envy impoverished their lives, but the intended harm never came to Joseph. Envy is a boomerang-like weapon which hurts the attacker more than the attacked.

Haman, envious of the sage Mordecai, pulled political strings to do away with him. So intent was he on annihilating the object of his envy that in over-anxiety he built a gallows for Mordecai to hang on. His tragic story ended with these words, "So they hanged Haman on the gallows that he had prepared for Mordecai . . ." (Esther 7:10).

How many of you have been hanged on the gallows that you made for some other person? Many a man has died on the gallows of envy that he had prepared for another. Look around you! Right in your own community you know people who have been resentful towards others, have been cynical about God and religion, or rebellious toward their neighbors. I defy you to show me an envious man who is a happy man. The

moment he began to build a gallows of envy—
he became spiritually dead.

Why is envy so great a sin? Was it just a whim
of God to denounce it? Did He arbitrarily forbid it just to make us miserable? Certainly not!
God is interested in our total and complete development. We are told in III John 2, "Beloved,
I wish above all things that thou mayest prosper
and be in health, even as thy soul prospereth."

Jealousy was one of the sins of Lucifer before
he was transformed into Satan. He was jealous
of God's position and determined that he was
going to dethrone God and put himself in God's
place. Therefore God hates envy and jealousy.
One of the sins that caused the death of Christ
was jealousy. "For envy, they delivered him"
(Mark 15:10).

The Pharisees and Sadducees were jealous of
the attention that Christ received. They were
envious of the great crowds that flocked to hear
Him, and because the people had made some-
what of a hero of Christ. Their jealousy burned
as flames of fire in their hearts. They counselled
together how they could put Him to death. The

Pharisees and Sadducees were not on very good terms, and on most points and issues there was no agreement. However, because their jealousy was so great, they pooled their resources in order to stop Jesus. They forgot their own differences because their jealous hearts were out of control. Jealousy takes many forms and many deviations, but it is hated by God and helps destroy all that are guilty of it.

Envy is also forbidden because it destroys spiritual health. Envy is a devastating symptom of this thing called "original sin," which we all have. Don't think you are alone in possessing it. Everyone has it, to a greater or lesser degree. Even Paul the Apostle, who warned Christians so sternly against it, once had a great amount of it. His was spiritual envy. He was jealous of the new sect called Christians, and his envy blazed up in vehement wrath. He went everywhere persecuting and destroying them; but in the face of a Christian named Stephen, at whose stoning he had officiated, Paul saw a Light which he had never seen before. He found this same Light on the Damascus road. His envy was changed to fervent love and unrestrained joy. Paul, bitter, cynical and envious, found a new zest in life when he turned from his envy and began serving the Saviour.

If you were to find the germs of tuberculosis lurking in your body, you would spare no time, effort or money in ruling them out. And yet, many people are afflicted with this deadly, venomous envy and they are doing nothing about it! In the eyes of God it is as ugly and deadly as open immorality. It is one of the seventeen fleshly sins mentioned by Paul in Galatians and ranks with adultery, murder, fornication and drunkenness. It is more prevalent than any of these, though the pulpit too seldom warns about its power to destroy. Though it is not forbidden by law, this vice which has infiltrated our modern life is sharply condemned by God. We are told in James 5:9, "Grudge not one against another . . . lest ye be condemned: behold the judge standeth before the door."

Envy is also forbidden because it takes the joy, happiness and contentment out of living. It is impossible to know serenity and contentment as long as jealousy is in one's heart. I have seen many lives filled with bitterness, hardness, frustration, confusion and even physical ailments as a direct result of jealousy. Jealousy takes away the effectiveness of one's work and can certainly destroy one's service for God. It causes all types of physical disorders because of the nervous tension that it brings on.

Envy isolates one from fellowship with God. There is no possibility that a person can be received into fellowship with God if he has envy in his heart. If you are not a Christian and have never given your heart and life to Christ, it is one of the symptoms of the basic sin that separates you and your God. You must repent of sin and receive Christ as Saviour before you can receive a new nature and victory over envy. If you are a Christian and have jealousy in your heart, then it means that you are out of fellowship with Christ and do not have the thrill and secret of victorious living. Since God loathes and abhors envy, He cannot bless you as long as you cling to it.

Shakespeare was close to this truth when he

said, "No, not the hangman's axe bears half the keenness of thy sharp envy."

It erodes through the soil of the soul, marooning the man who indulges in it on an island of selfishness. In the chemistry of the spirit, no sin is so devastating, no sin can so quickly mar the sweet fellowship between man and God.

Envy isolates one from his fellow man. The envious man is destined to live alone. In the end, it becomes spiritual leprosy, isolating him from friends and fellowship with God.

Those who are guilty of this sin are going to be judged. We are warned in the Bible that some day we shall stand before the judgment of God and give an account of all the secret thoughts of jealousy and envy that we have harbored in our heart.

Many of you are asking, "How can I get rid of this devastating sin which robs me of soul, health and happiness?"

First, recognize that you have it. Doctors say that a case well diagnosed is half cured. Stop blaming others for your failures. Take inventory of your own soul, and take positive action to get rid of the sins which have beset you. To admit a fault does not make you smaller—on the contrary, it makes you appear bigger in the eyes of others.

Secondly, confess your sin to God and renounce it. In I John 1:9 we read, "If we confess . . . He will forgive." James 5:16 says, "Confess your faults . . . that ye may be healed." Many a person has started on the road to spiritual recovery by a straightforward confession to God. Confess your sins, renounce them, repent of them.

Thirdly, open your heart to the regenerating grace of Christ. Envy cannot be overcome in your strength. Paul had learned the secret when he said in Philippians 4:13, "I can do all things through Christ which strengtheneth me." As the Christ-nature unfolds in your life, you will find that the old strivings, the old envyings, are more easily conquered. You will discover the full meaning of the words, "And they that are Christ's have crucified the flesh with the affections and lusts" (Galatians 5:24) and that "The fruit of the Spirit is love, joy, peace, longsuffering . . ." (Galatians 5:22).

Fourthly, ask the Holy Spirit to come into your heart to give you victory. It is possible to ". . . reckon ye also yourselves to be dead indeed unto sin, but alive unto God" (Romans 6:11). "The fruit of the Spirit is love . . ." (Galatians 5:22) and where love dwells in all of its fullness, there is no room for envy and jealousy.

You can have complete and unqualified victory by surrendering completely to Christ.

4

IMPURITY

The sin of impurity at the outset does not appear ugly and venomous. It comes in the guise of beauty, symmetry and desirability. There is nothing repulsive about it. Satan clothes his goddess of lust as an angel of love, and her appearance has deceived the strongest of men. "After all, it's a natural instinct," says the rationalist. "This is God-endowed." But wait a minute—the Bible says in Proverbs 6:32, 33, "But whosoever committeth adultery with a woman lacketh understanding: he that doeth it destroyeth his own soul. A wound and dishonour shall he get; and his reproach shall not be wiped away."

God hates this sin of impurity. It has caused nations to fall. It has over and over again ruined the sanctity of the home. It has hindered the health and development of the personality, and it has caused the spiritual impotence of thousands. It has filled our divorce courts, made thousands of innocent children homeless and has wrecked the hope of the bright tomorrow for many a young person.

Impurity is one of the most revolting of sins because it twists and distorts one of God's most precious gifts to man—human love—and drags it down to the level of the beast. But despite its heinousness, it is the most prevalent of all of Satan's contrivances. Its raucous sound falls upon our ears throughout the day in the form of filthy stories, suggestive remarks and open vulgarity. It bids for our attention from the pages of our magazines, the television screen and from the lewd play in the theater.

Impurity obviously has a better press agent than purity. Purity by the rank and file is considered smug, but impurity is considered smart. This is the biggest "bill of goods" that the devil ever put over on the human race. In selling "sex" wholesale the momentary thrill is played up, but the consequences of this vicious sin are played down. Satan fails to speak of the remorse, the futility, the loneliness and the spiritual devastation which goes hand in hand with immorality. Nothing is said of the broken homes, the shattered lives, the fevered brains and the diseased bodies which result from living impurely.

Ask the "shadow girls" in London, the "B" girls in New Orleans, or the common prostitutes in Tokyo if it pays to be impure! Ask the often-divorced woman whose name is continually in our newspapers if a change of mates has brought any change of heart or inner peace! A newspaper story about a famous American woman who has been married four times said, "She looked haggard, tired and worn." It remarked that the radiant glow had gone from her face, and she seemed bored and unhappy with life. The artificiality of the outward appearance of these women is a symbol of their inner sham and emptiness. Ask the incurables in our hospitals and sanatoriums, who are paying physically for breaking the seventh commandment, if sin brings happiness! As they watch the sands of time run out, and as the folly of their youth takes its toll, their voices say eloquently, "The wages of sin is death" (Romans 6:23).

The sin of immorality is one of hell's keenest weapons for the destruction of souls, and Satan has used it effectively from the dawn of creation to this present hour. It never seems to lose its subtlety at the beginning or its destructiveness at the end. Its beauty is exceeded only by its deadliness.

A well-known American writer wrote an article entitled, "I Am Sick of Sex." By this she meant that she was sick of seeing it everywhere. She said, "Whether I look at a newsstand or watch my television screen, it's there before me." But apparently millions of Americans do not agree with this woman. A magazine editor told me that in order to sell magazines he had to put "sex" on the front cover. In my opinion sex is probably America's greatest sin. It has gripped and paralyzed our youth until a recent survey indicated that six out of every ten young women have had sex experience by the time they have reached the age of twenty-one.

During the past few years we have been taught that morals were relative and not absolute. Humanism and behaviorism laughed at the Ten Commandments and the idea of God. They taught that man was only an animal, and our young people were urged to give free expression to their passions and feelings. Our high school and college young people were told that what was wrong in the puritanical age of yesterday is no longer wrong. The sin of "scarlet" turned to a mild "pink," and a young man and woman who tried to live clean and pure lives were laughed at and scorned even by some educational authorities. No wonder our country has plunged into an unprecedented immoral spree that threatens the very structure of our society!

There are three facts about the sin of impurity which I would like for you to notice. *First,* the sin of impurity marks. In the days of slavery a slave could be identified by the marks of his master. When men become mastered by sin, it is inescapable that the marks of sin are upon them. The reddened eyes and bloated cheeks of the alcoholic, the nervous twitch of the dope fiend, the lewd stare of the impure, and the haughty look of the proud are all imprints of inner wickedness. Immorality, which is the sin of perversion and unnaturalness, has a way of making those who harbor it unnatural appearing. The shifty eye, the embarrassed blush, the suggestive glance—these are all marks of the impure. They are the outward signs of inward impurity.

But the outward marks are slight compared to the blemishes which impurity etches on the personality and upon the soul. Guilt complexes and bad consciences are fashioned in the fires of lustful passion. Out of unbalanced practices of impurity grow phobias which alarm even our most skilled psychiatrists. But worse than all, impurity mars the souls. The Bible says in Galatians 5:19, "The works of the flesh are these; adultery, fornication, uncleanness and lasciviousness." The Bible says that the sin of impurity is the result of the deceitfulness of sin. The Bible teaches that "There is none that doeth good, no not one" (Psalm 14:3), and that the entire human race has been tainted by the disease of sin. The Bible also teaches that those who are guilty of this sin of impurity shall not inherit the kingdom of God. Jesus interpreted the Seventh Commandment which says, "Thou shalt not commit adultery," when He said, "Whosoever looketh upon a woman to lust after her hath committed adultery with her already . . ." (Matthew 5:28). Jesus said that a person can be guilty of this sin by thought and word, as well as deed. There are thousands today who are guilty, whose souls have been marred by the sin of impurity, and who have become separated from God because of this besetting sin.

Next, impurity mocks or deceives. Paul, writing to Titus, indicates that even he knew the deceitfulness of immorality before he came to know Jesus Christ. He said in Titus 3:3, "For we ourselves also were sometimes foolish, disobedient, deceived, serving divers lusts and pleasures . . ." It has deceived kings, prophets, sages and saints. Do not think for one moment that you are immune to its blight! Even the wise Solomon, who through experience had every reason to know, said, "Fools make a mock of sin" (Proverbs 14:9).

Too many people underestimate the power of impurity. Samson toyed with it, made sport of it and thought he had it under control, but in the end it controlled him and ruined his life. David, chosen of God, came under its subtle spell and in a moment of weakness was deceived by the overcoming powers of impurity—and he was years climbing back to God up the steep stairway of repentance. Homes have been lost in a fleeting moment of weakness, kingdoms have been bartered for a transient pleasure, and an eternal heritage has been squandered for an hour of hell's diversion.

Impurity mocks those who harbor it in their hearts. Impurity mocks when its harvest is gathered. In Galatians 6:7 and 8 we read, "Be not deceived, God is not mocked; for whatsoever a man soweth, that shall he also reap. For he that soweth to his flesh shall of the flesh reap corruption . . ."

Impurity, when it is finished brings forth remorse. Some of the most miserable men I know are those who are haunted by the memory of the wasted, wanton years of impurity. God is willing to forgive them, but they are not willing and able to forgive themselves. The magnitude of their sin has grown through the years, and it has born its fruit of regret and remorse. They have sown to the flesh, and of the flesh have reaped corruption. Their impurity mocks them, haunts them and derides them. Like every other device of the Devil, it has taken away from them all that is good and has given them nothing in return. Satan drives a hard bargain!

Then, impurity masters. The Bible says in Romans 6:16, "Know ye not that to whom ye yield yourselves servants to obey, his servants ye are to whom ye obey?" Many people are mastered by impurity because they have given themselves to impurity.

A medical doctor in London accepted Christ during our first Greater London Crusade. Before his conversion he was ruled by animal passion and was dedicated to a life of unchastity.

His reading room was crammed full of salacious and suggestive literature and photographs. But after his conversion he was repulsed by the thought of impure practices and promptly gathered up all his lewd literature, carried it to a London bridge and cast it into the Thames River. Having experienced the new birth, he yielded himself to a new Master—even Christ. He became one of the most active Christian laymen in the city of London, and everyone respects him.

Thousands of people are held in the iron grip of impurity and immorality. Sin, because they have obeyed it and yielded to it, has become their master. "Whosoever committeth sin is the servant of sin" (John 8:34). They are conscious that what they are doing is wrong, but they are powerless to break with their impurity. Their sin has lost its keen edge of enjoyment and has settled down to a kind of bondage. It has become their master! Once they had sin—but now their sin has them!

Is there any hope for those who are held in the grip of impurity? Ah yes, there is. Mary Magdalene, the woman at Jacob's well and the woman taken in adultery can all sing in unison:

> There is a fountain filled with blood,
> Drawn from Immanuel's veins.
> And sinners plunged beneath that flood,
> Lose all their guilty stains.

There is a crimson cure for the scarlet sin.

When the adulteress was brought to Jesus by the Pharisees, they demanded that she be stoned and destroyed. Jesus stooped down and with His finger wrote on the ground. Whatever He wrote (and it well might have been the Ten Commandments) made them leave one by one. Jesus stood alone with the woman and He asked, "Hath no man condemned thee?" She said, "No man, Lord." Jesus said unto her, "Neither do I condemn thee. Go, and sin no more" (John 8:3-11). This impure woman was the symbol of all those who are held in the grip of impurity. She had sinned—yes, but "all have sinned, and come short of the glory of God" (Romans 3:23).

Christ can do only one thing with sin. He does not condone it, nor condemn it—He forgives it. We read in John 3:17 that "God sent not his

Son into the world to condemn the world, but that the world through him might be saved." When Christ died on the Cross, He died for the sin of impurity as well as for other sins. Actually, impurity is only a symptom of the "original sin" that David said he was born in and shapen in. Every person who is born of woman is born a sinner. There is only one place of forgiveness, and that is at the foot of the Cross where we come by repentance and faith to receive Christ as Saviour. It is only on the grounds of the death of His Son that God can forgive sin.

If you will bring your life to Jesus Christ, God will forgive every sin you have ever committed. He can even forget that you have ever sinned. You can be justified in His presence and cleansed of all impurity. Not only so, but He gives victory over it! He said to the woman, "Go, and sin no more." There are many of you who say, "I've tried a thousand times, but it has an unbreakable grip on me." Yes, but Jesus gave hope to this woman that He could give her victory over future sin. He never told anyone to do something but that He gave the power to do it.

You, too, can determine by God's grace that you will never commit this sin again. You have no strength of your own, but Christ will come into your heart and give you supernatural strength and power to resist the fearful temptation of passion. For the sin of impurity your conscience goads you, your memory haunts you, and society condemns you— but Jesus Christ will save you. He can be yours. Confess your sins, receive Him and let Him cleanse you and make you a new person.

5

GLUTTONY

I know a man who weighs nearly three hundred pounds. He eats more than anyone I have ever known. I had breakfast with him not long ago when he ate an entire lemon chiffon pie. When I mentioned that he should be losing weight, he gave a hearty laugh and put an extra pat of butter on his toast. He is actually digging his grave with his knife and fork. This man is guilty of the sin the Bible calls "gluttony."

During recent years in America our standard of living has been rising. Most Americans are now living at ease with more leisure time on their hands and more food to eat than any people in the history of the world. As a result — creeping materialism, the cult of comfort, is growing by leaps and bounds in America. Communism, a few years back considered our greatest foe, must take a back seat to this philosophy of "prosperity and plenty" as public enemy number one, which advocates ease and luxury, and preaches that men can live by bread alone. Appetite is its god; the merchandise counter, its altar. Its creed is plenty, and its heaven is comfort. In an era of economic prosperity, there is a grave danger of the sin of indulging our fleshly appetites and yielding to inordinate eating, drinking and revelry.

Gluttony is one of the seven deadly sins and has been placed by the church fathers right alongside pride, envy and impurity. It is a sin that most of us commit, but few of us mention. It is one of the most prevalent sins among Christians. Although there are no laws on our statute books which forbid gluttony, it is strongly denounced in the Bible.

Many people guilty of gluttony are quick to condemn others for their sins. They can readily detect a mote of impurity in the other man but remain ignorant of the beam of overindulgence in themselves. It is easy for a man who surfeits and stuffs his body with needless delicacies to look at the man who overdrinks and say like the Pharisee of old, "Lord, I thank Thee that I am not as other men are: extortioners, unjust, adulterers, or even as this Publican" (Luke 18:11). It is easy for a man who is enslaved by his stomach to condemn the man who is enslaved by drink. But in God's sight, sin is sin.

Gluttony, surfeiting and overindulgence are condemned as sharply as the other deadly sins which beset men. Philippians 3:19 reads, "Whose end is destruction, whose God is their belly, and whose glory is in their shame, who mind earthly things." Here gluttony is identified with materialism, "who mind earthly things."

Gluttony is a sin, first, because it is a physical expression of the philosophy of materialism. It laughs at righteous restraint and scorns temperance and decency. It cries, "Eat, drink and be merry, for tomorrow we die." It makes no room for God and has no consideration for eternity. It lives for the present, and its philosophy is, "You live only once, so live it up."

Jesus gave us a classic example of a man who lived for this life only. In his prosperity he said, "I will pull down my barns and build greater; and there will I bestow all my fruits and my goods. And I will say to my soul, Soul, thou hast much goods laid up for many years; take thine ease, eat, drink, and be merry" (Luke 12:18, 19). His philosophy was little different from our materialistic philosophy of today. Build bigger . . . take it easier . . . drink more . . . eat more . . . enjoy life more.

We hear this philosophy blaring out of our radio and television sets from morning till night. The accent is on comfort, ease and the satisfying of our appetites. We see it pictured in our magazines. Everywhere we are encouraged to easier living and more and better food — with the accent on the things of this world. Temperance, restraint and self-discipline are being forgotten in the rush toward ease and plenty. This generation, shot through with the materialistic philosophy, is trying in vain to drink its way to happiness, fight its way to peace, spend its way to prosperity and enjoy its way to heaven. How easy it is in this day to fill our minds with rubbish, our stomachs with trash — and starve our souls. God has said in Deuteronomy 8:3, "Man shall not live by bread alone, but by every word that proceedeth out of the mouth of God."

Gluttony is a perversion of a natural, God-given appetite. We must fix in our minds the fact that sin is not always flagrant and open transgression. It is often the perversion and distortion of natural, normal desires and appetites. Love is often distorted into lust. Self-respect too often is perverted into godless ambition. When a God-given, normal hunger is extended greedily into abnormality so that it harms the body, dulls the mind, and stultifies the soul, it becomes sin. In Proverbs 23:21 we read, "For the drunkard and the glutton shall come to poverty; and drowsiness shall clothe a man with rags."

The gratification of our fleshly appetites is not to receive first importance in our lives. Jesus said, "Take no thought saying, What shall we eat? or, What shall we drink? . . . But seek ye first the kingdom of God, and His righteousness; and all these things shall be added unto you" (Matthew 6:31, 33).

Most of us have disregarded Jesus' warning about putting our fleshly appetites first. Too many of us spend our lives in the pursuit of the material, crowding Christ out altogether; and then in the last frenzied, hurried moment of life we cry, "God have mercy on my soul!" I ask you: is it fair, is it intelligent, to wait until the last second of life upon this earth to transact life's most urgent business — settling your account with God? Of course it is not fair, and I seriously doubt the genuineness of such a deathbed repentance. God may give a man a chance on his deathbed to repent of sin if the man has never been warned and has never heard the plan of salvation clearly explained. But to a man who has deliberately rejected Christ and continued in his sins, there is little hope that he can find peace with God in his last hours. The Bible warns that a day will come when a person will seek Him but will not find Him, and call on Him but He will not hear.

Many people do not look upon gluttony as a vicious sin, and yet it is condemned from one end of the Bible to the other. When we go to the table, we show no self-restraint, no self-discipline; and we eat our way not only to the grave, but to hell and destruction as well. Of course, gluttony is not only the sin of overeating. It can be the sin of drinking, of dissipation or of staying up too late night after night for pleasure and amusement, losing needless sleep in order to satisfy ambition, greed, or lust. Gluttony can also be indulged in by married couples who have not used self-restraint and temperance in their relations with each other. They have overindulged, and as a result their bodies as well as their minds and souls suffer. The Bible demands that in all things we are to be temperate, and we are not to abuse any God-given privilege.

Gluttony is the epitome of human selfishness. It is destined to be judged like any other deadly sin. God says in Amos 6:4, "Woe unto them . . . that lie upon beds of ivory, and stretch themselves upon their couches, and eat the lambs out of the flock, and the calves out of the midst of the stall; that drink wine in bowls, and anoint themselves with the chief ointments . . ."

Three-fifths of the world live in squalor, misery and hunger. Too long have the privileged few exploited and ignored the underprivileged millions of the world. Our selfishness is at long last catching up with us. Unless we begin to act, to share, and to do something about this great army of starving humanity, God will judge us.

Communism, with its multiplied millions of adherents, promises to help the helpless. Unless Christians break with their selfishness and begin to help these millions of starving people out of their misery, they will turn to the only other alternative — Communism.

Even though this is an era of prosperity there is shocking evidence of selfishness and greed on every hand. Who knows but what God has permitted this prosperity to come that we may share it with the suffering and needy, and thus lure them away from Communism by our love and compassion! I John 3:17 speaks for itself — "Whoso hath this world's good, and seeth his brother have need, and shutteth up his bowels of compassion from him, how dwelleth the love of God in him?"

We are not only to witness for Christ with our lips, but with our hands — hands laden with food for the hungry, clothes for the naked; and water for the thirsty. We read in I John 3:18, "My little children, let us not love in word, neither in tongue; but in deed and in truth." Shame, O shame, that in an hour when millions are hanging in the balance between Christian love and the clutches of materialism, we should be given to surfeiting, gluttony and drunkenness! May God awaken us out of our sinful stupor before it is too late!

Gluttony is sinful because it defiles the body which is the temple of the Holy Spirit. Our bodies were not created to be dissipated and abused by sin — they were created by God Himself and were intended to be the dwelling of His Spirit. The Bible says in I Corinthians 6:19 and 20, "What? know ye not that your body is the temple of the Holy Ghost which is in you, which ye have of God, and ye are not your own. For ye are bought with a price: therefore glorify God in your body, and in your spirit, which are God's." Any sin against the body is a sin against God, for He created us and we are the work of His hands.

The Romans, before the fall of Rome, were given to three major sins: gluttony, drunkenness and immorality. They dug their graves with their teeth, killed themselves by illicit indulgence and embalmed themselves with alcohol. It is said that at their sumptuous banquets it was a common sight for men to rush to the windows, eject the contents of their stomachs and then return to the banquet table for further surfeiting. No individual, nor nation, which is given to surfeiting, drunkenness and gluttony can expect the smile and blessing of God. Rome fell because she overstuffed her body and starved her soul. Millions with excessive appetites and greedy souls, like a dumb animal in new clover, can cast aside all reason and propriety and eat until they die. We read in I Timothy 5:6 that "she that liveth in pleasure is dead while she liveth." Unbalanced living, leaving God out of the picture, inevitably leads to spiritual suicide.

The fact that in an era of record prosperity our psychiatrists, our counselors and our ministers are working night and day in a frantic effort to relieve the mentally and spiritually distressed, proves that we have attained economic prosperity, but are starving ourselves spiritually. We have undoubtedly prospered materially, but out of all proportion to our soul development.

Two sides of our nature cry for attention. The body demands food, water and air, and there is nothing sinful about our satisfying its demands. However, when we cater to the appetites of the flesh to the exclusion and neglect of our souls, we become guilty of the sin of gluttony.

The prodigal son is a classic example of this common human error. He fell a prey to materialism. The end result of godless materialism is found in the words: "And when he had spent all, there arose a mighty famine in the land; and he began to be in want" (Luke 15:14). Materialism spends itself — so does gluttony, pride and impurity. They never satisfy because they are slanted toward only one aspect of our nature. The soul can only find sustenance and rest in God.

The thieves on either side of Christ at Calvary represented all that is sinful and loathesome in mankind. They had lived selfishly, greedily and murderously. But one of them, repentant and broken, had the faith to turn to Jesus and confess Him as Lord. "Lord, remember me," he cried. Christ, ever ready to save, even during the sublime act of redemption, turned and assured him saying, "This day shalt thou be with me in Paradise" (Luke 23:42, 43).

There are thousands who have lived selfishly and godlessly, and are wondering what they can do to undo the past and change the future course of their lives. They can come by repentance of sin and faith to the Cross and receive Christ as their Lord and Saviour. He will forgive the past and give the power of self-discipline, temperance and restraint in the days ahead.

A woman who called me on the phone during one of our crusades said, "I have a sin that haunts me day and night. I cannot get victory, and yet I've tried a thousand times. I'm guilty of the sin of gluttony." This was the first time that I had ever had anyone come to me and confess that they were guilty of this sin. I have had many people laughingly tell me that they have "overstuffed," but few consider it a sin. Yet the Bible is specific in stating that gluttony is one of the worst of all sins, and the church has said that it is one of the seven deadly sins.

This woman came to the Cross and found forgiveness of the past and victory over gluttony. You, too, can receive Christ, and He will transform your life and give you a power that is beyond yourself to help you to overcome the sins of intemperance, gluttony and surfeiting. He can give you complete and abiding victory.

6

SLOTHFULNESS

Some Bible teachers suggest that the sin of slothfulness is not so much a sin of the present era in which we live as it was in the ancient world. However, as I studied my Bible for this message, I became convinced that it is one of the great sins that is being committed in America today.

Webster's dictionary defines sloth as "a disinclination to action or labor; sluggishness, laziness, idleness and indolence."

In theological language it carries with it the idea of not only laziness in spiritual things, but apathy and inactivity in the practice of our Christianity.

The Bible has a great deal to say about the

blighting, deadening, damning sin of slothfulness. It says in Proverbs 19:15, "Slothfulness casteth into a deep sleep; and an idle soul shall suffer hunger." Again the Bible says in Proverbs 21:25, "The desire of the slothful killeth him; for his hands refuse to labor."

The Bible indicates that the sin of slothfulness engenders a negative kind of life which is stagnant and ineffective and which renders a person unworthy of being a follower of Jesus Christ. Spiritual laziness is not only a sin against God — it is a sin against yourself. It measures the distance between what you ought to be and what you actually are. It shows the difference between the person you are and the person you could be.

Slothfulness is the destroyer of opportunity and the murderer of souls. It kills stealthily and silently, but it kills just the same.

The slothful man is like driftwood floating downward with the current — effortlessly and heedlessly. The easy way is the popular way, the broad way, the way of the crowd. It takes no effort, no strength, no manhood to be lost.

A drifting boat always goes downstream — never up. A drifting, slothful soul inevitably is drifting toward an eternity of destruction.

Many a man has lost his life in an automobile accident, not because he was a bad driver, but because he was a good driver — asleep. Many persons are fighting losing battles spiritually, not because they are really bad, but because they are spiritually slothful, sleepy and drowsy. Ephesians 5:14 declares, "Awake, thou that sleepest, and arise from the dead, and Christ shall give thee light."

Many persons have lost their health and their life, not because they have abused their bodies by sin, but because they have neglected their bodies. They were just too lazy to take care of themselves.

Slothfulness reaps its annual harvest of thousands of deaths on the highways, thousands of physical breakdowns, and a staggering amount of suffering and misery across the world.

The sin of doing nothing has been called in the Scriptures the sin of omission — which is just as dangerous as the sin of commission.

You do not have to do anything to be lost — just be slothful about your soul — just do nothing. Jesus said that it is easy to be lost. He said, "Wide is the gate, and broad is the way that leadeth to destruction, and many there be which go in thereat" (Matthew 7:14).

In the parable of the talents given by Jesus, we read not only of the reward of the faithful servant, but of the judgment of the slothful servant. His judgment for doing nothing was as great as the judgment of those that had committed adultery and murder. Matthew 25:26-30 records His sentence: "Thou wicked and slothful servant . . . take therefore the talent from him . . . and cast ye the unprofitable servant into outer darkness: there shall be weeping and gnashing of teeth." The unprofitable servant had done no outward wrong — he simply was too slothful to carry out the responsibility which had been assigned to him. His sin was the sin of slothfulness, the sin of doing nothing.

The chief sin of the ten virgins was not immorality, lying or cheating — it was slothfulness. They simply neglected to provide themselves with oil. They were judged, not for flagrant sin, but for laziness and unfaithfulness. When the bridegroom came, the door of opportunity slammed shut, and the voice of God echoed in judgment, "I know ye not" (Matthew 25:12).

In every area of life the slothful person is the loser. The slothful, lazy student who spends his time loafing in the campus drug store can never hope to be on the honor roll. Diplomas are usually awarded for faithful work and diligent study — not for native talent or ability. It is usually the person who is willing to work who wins the applause of his professors. On the farm, in business, in the school, in the shop and in every area of our lives, slothfulness is judged and faithfulness is rewarded.

Slothfulness is a destroyer in everyday life. On its account, lives have been lost, cities have been ravaged by fire, and homes have been broken. It has kept the hobo from a life of respectability, the prostitute from living a life of purity, and the thief from being honest.

Someone has aptly said, "It isn't the thing

you do, friend; but the thing you leave undone, that gives you a bit of a heartache at the setting of the sun."

The encouraging word we might have spoken to a discouraged friend, the helpful deed that would have made someone's burden a little lighter, the bit of money pressed lovingly into the hand of the needy — these are the neglected things that bring remorse and rob others of the help they need. When through slothfulness we fail to do that loving deed, Jesus' words of judgment ring in our ears, "Inasmuch as ye did it not unto one of the least of these, ye did it not unto me" (Matthew 25:45).

There are thousands of people who are slothful about church-going. They like to sleep late on Sunday morning or go out for a game of golf. Others like to sit at home and read the newspaper and rationalize that they can hear a sermon by radio or watch a religious program on television. They think by thus doing that they have discharged their religious responsibility.

There are others who are slothful about their prayer life. Paul said that we are to "pray without ceasing" (I Thessalonians 5:17). He meant that we were to be in the attitude of prayer at all times. Because we are lazy and slothful, our prayer life is neglected, and thus our spiritual resources are dried up.

I have found that if I leave in the morning without spending a period of time in prayer, the day is completely wrong and troubles and problems mount.

Most of us would rather have that extra wink of sleep than spend fifteen minutes in prayer with God in the morning.

We allow everything else to interfere with our appointment with God. If you had an appointment to see the President of the United States or the Queen of Great Britain at a certain hour, I dare say you would not be tardy or late. You would probably be ahead of time and deeply concerned about how you were dressed and what you would say to so distinguished a person. Yet we are continually late and tardy in our daily appointment with God. We never prepare our minds for the period of prayer. We usually give God the odd moment or the last moment before we retire, when we are so sleepy that we cannot keep our minds on what we are doing. We are guilty of the sin of slothfulness.

There are thousands of Christians who are guilty of slothfulness in Bible reading. I Peter 2:2 teaches that we are to "desire the sincere milk of the Word, that ye may grow thereby." The reason many Christians are not growing is that they are not reading the Bible, and the reason they are not reading the Bible is that they are too slothful. The Psalmist said that he meditated in the laws of God day and night; and as a result, God's words were like honeycomb to his heart and soul. Many of you are wondering why you do not have the thrill and joy of Christian experience that you know others have. It is because you are not reading the Bible. You are guilty of the terrible sin of slothfulness. You are leaving undone those things you ought to have done.

There are many others that are slothful about witnessing for Christ. How long has it been since you spoke to a soul about Christ? How long has it been since you won another person to a saving knowledge of Jesus Christ? There are scores of people that you contact every day that need the Saviour, and yet not one word has ever escaped your lips trying to win them to know Christ. You are guilty of the sin of slothfulness, and others will be lost because you are guilty of this sin.

There are others who are slothful in the way they live. It is a sin to be slothful in dress and in conversation. It is sinful to be slothful in the ordinary courtesies of everyday living.

The sin of slothfulness extends into many areas, such as: being slothful about your driving habits on the highway, thus endangering the lives of others; being slothful about your personal cleanliness, which is next to Godliness; being slothful about the smile that should be upon the face of every Christian at all times, no matter what the circumstances; being slothful about helping those that are in need in your neighborhood; being slothful about giving to charity, so that the unfortunate and the underprivileged do not have the necessities of life.

There are others that are slothful in giving of their tithes and offerings to the kingdom of God. If the average business kept books the way the average Christian keeps books in relation to his debts and gifts to God, it would go bankrupt within a few days.

There are thousands of Christians who are slumbering and keeping their mouths shut while the world is in desperate need of the Gospel of Jesus Christ. The Bible warns in Isaiah 56: 10 that "his watchmen are blind: they are all ignorant, they are all dumb dogs, they cannot bark; sleeping, lying down, loving to slumber." Romans 12:11 advises us to be "not slothful in business; fervent in spirit, serving the Lord." There are many ways that you can serve Christ, no matter what your circumstances.

The New Testament continually warns against the sin of slothfulness, "That ye be not slothful, but followers of them who through faith and patience inherit the promises" (Hebrews 6:12).

Martin Luther wrote in one of his sermons:

The Devil held a great anniversary at which his emissaries were convened to report the results of their several missions.

"I let loose the wild beasts of the desert," said one, "on a caravan of Christians; and their bones are now bleaching in the sands."

"What of that?" said the Devil. "Their souls were all saved."

"I drove the east wind," said another, "against a ship freighted with Christians, and they were all drowned."

"What of that?" said the Devil. "Their souls were saved."

"For ten years I tried to get a person to be at ease about his soul, and at last I succeeded, and he is ours," said another.

Then the Devil shouted, and the night stars of hell sang for joy.

The sin of slothfulness and criminal spiritual neglect has probably done as much to populate hell as the vicious sins we hear so much about. It seems so harmless, so innocent, and yet its venom is more deadly to the spirit of man than some of the most hideous sins to which men are addicted.

The worst thing that slothfulness does is to rob a man of spiritual purpose — the power of Christian decision. In stupidity and indolence, this spiritual drowsiness renders him incapable of choosing Christ. He may give mental assent to the truth, he may even know the doctrines of religion; but he is incapable of positive action. The road is clear before him. He knows the way he should go, but slothfulness has made his will soft and irresponsible. This sin must be confessed like any other. James 4:17 says, "To him that knoweth to do good, and doeth it not, to him it is sin."

In the crowd of people who gathered around the Cross of Christ were those who were committing the sin of slothfulness. Even though Christ, the Son of God, was dying, Matthew 27:36 says that "sitting down, they watched Him there." Such indifference! Such unthinkable sloth! But just before Jesus breathed His last breath, He looked at the sinners all around

Him — the thieves, the murderers, the gamblers, the hypocrites, the profane, the immoral, the proud, the envious, the greedy, the gluttonous and the slothful; and He said, "Father, forgive them, for they know not what they do" (Luke 23:34). In that moment, the Lamb of God (to everyone who would believe) took away the sins of the world. By that redemptive, consummate act, He opened up the way to heaven.

Eternal life is within reach of everyone. The Saviour is as near as your yielded will, or He is as far away as you want Him to be. Your own stubborn, slothful spirit is your greatest hindrance to letting Him come into your heart.

7

AVARICE

Avarice, the close relative of covetousness, is probably the parent of more evil than all the other sins. In fact, I Timothy 6:10 says that the "love of money is the root of all evil." Men driven by avarice have robbed, assaulted, attacked, embezzled, slandered and murdered. Covetousness was one of the first sins to raise its venomous head in the Garden of Eden. In Genesis 3:6 we read that "when the woman saw that the tree was good for food, and pleasant to the eyes, and a tree to be desired, she took of the fruit thereof, and did eat." This sin of avarice is as much a part of the natural man as breathing. From babyhood to old age it motivates our actions and shapes our behavior patterns.

It has also forced its way into our ethical ideology. Such catch phrases as "self preservation is man's first instinct," "self protection is the first law of life," "look out for number one" are all adages of avarice.

The Garden of Eden was a place of indescribable beauty until the sin of avarice crept in. After that it was an eerie swamp with a flaming sword of judgment which turned every way. Life can never be hallowed with the bliss of Eden, and man can never know the fellowship of God until he finds victory over the blighting sin of greed and selfishness. No sin can rob life of its beauty and radiance as thoroughly as the sin of avarice.

Scan through the pages of the Bible and note the trail of abject misery which this deadly sin has made through human history. It was an unholy, unnatural lust for selfish gain that caused King Ahab to covet Naboth's vineyard and eventually to murder to achieve his avaricious end. But the voice of God came to

Ahab, saying, "In the place where dogs licked the blood of Naboth shall dogs lick thy blood" (I Kings 21:19).

Avarice first claims our souls, then seals our destiny. Ahab little dreamed that the innocent seed of greed in his heart would in the end bring forth a harvest of death and judgment. Joseph's brothers sowed the tiny seed of avarice and greed when they sold their godly brother into slavery, but little did they foresee the harvest of famine and misery which they were to reap when avarice came into full bloom.

The rich man of whom Jesus spoke sowed a crop of selfishness and greed, and Jesus said that it brought forth plentifully. This rich man soon came to know the futility which comes from full barns, full pockets, but an empty heart. He was soon to drop dead with a voice from heaven saying, "Thou fool, this night thy soul is required of thee" (Luke 12:20).

Judas, driven by avarice, sold his Lord for thirty pieces of silver but found out that life was not worth living without Him. Throwing the tarnished silver at the feet of the greedy men with whom he had made a poor bargain, he went out and hanged himself; but long before the life was choked out of the body, his soul was dead — it had been strangled by greed and avarice. To all the Ahabs, the Judases, the foolish men of every age who live selfishly and greedily, Christ says in Luke 12:21, "So is he that layeth up treasures for himself and is not rich toward God."

Avarice seeks more than its own in life. It cheats, robs, murders and slanders to achieve its desires. The Bible teaches that we are born with the sin of avarice. We read in Jeremiah 6:13 that "from the least of them, even unto the greatest of them, everyone is given to covetousness." Babies are born with selfish, grasping, greedy natures. Though they cannot make requirements known in words, they have a way of making their desires known.

I was in a home some time ago where the mother, the grandmother, the housekeeper and the father were running in every direction in a frantic effort to gratify the desires of a single baby. Even growing children are selfish by nature. "Daddy, what did you get me?" is as familiar a cry in my home as it is in yours.

Jeremiah said, "From the least of them even unto the greatest of them everyone is given to covetousness" (Jeremiah 6:13). As long as the prodigal son sang the song of "Give me," his lot was misery, want, loneliness and famine; but when he changed his song to "Forgive me," he found himself in a state of fellowship, comfort and plenty.

Charles Kingsley has said, "If you wish to be miserable, think about yourself: about what you want, what you like, what respect people ought to pay you — and then to you, nothing will be pure. You will spoil everything you touch. You will make misery for yourself out of everything good. You will be as wretched as you choose."

Covetousness has been rated in Romans 1:29 with the more open and vicious sins, "Being filled with all unrighteousness, fornication, wickedness, covetousness and maliciousness." In Romans 13:9 it is mentioned with murder, immorality, stealing and lying. This sin, which has stunted the spiritual development of so many people and has appeared so harmless, is considered in the Word of God as one of the most hideous and destructive of all Satan's tools. In fact, the Bible goes so far as to warn that a covetous man and a man guilty of avarice cannot inherit the kingdom of God (I Corinthians 6:10).

The Bible teaches that greed is idolatry. A piece of silver can be held so close to your eyes that you cannot see the sun, and the love of money can so fill your heart that God will be crowded out. In this age of materialism the consuming passion for material gain has made millions forget the words of Jesus in Mark 8:36, "What shall it profit a man if he gain the whole world and lose his own soul?" If our lives are to show a profit when our record books are balanced, there must be more than dollar signs written there.

The love of money corrodes the hearts of men, spoiling their happiness and setting them in conflict with one another. The lust of one country for the soil of another has thousands of times let loose war and pillage on innocent populations. The powerful have, in every age, under the sway of similar motives, plundered the goods and oppressed the persons of the weak. Employers down through the centuries have extracted the toll from laborers, even while their consciences told them that they were not paying wages commensurate with the work being done.

It was the sin of avarice that caused slavery and the suffering, misery and death that accompanied this plague of the human race. The love of money is what causes the robberies that we read about in our daily papers and often causes murder. It is the sin of avarice that causes a dairyman to put water in the milk and a farmer to put his best apples on top. It is avarice that causes a lawyer to lie and an operator on the stock market to swindle his clients.

The Roman fathers centuries ago used to say to their sons, "Get money honestly if you can, but in any case get money."

The great sin of America is greed and avarice. We are so bent on making money that we do not have time for God and spiritual exercise. Many businesses are kept open unnecessarily on Sunday, thus desecrating God's day in order to gain a few extra dollars. How many times I have asked men to go to church, and they have said they had to work. They are so busy making money they have no time for God. Americans do not realize that in their desire for ease, luxury and the making of money, they may soon lose all in the most horrifying and terrible destruction the world has ever known. I beg of you Americans, wake up before it's too late!

It is the sin of avarice which causes gamblers to have fever in their blood and drives them on, recklessly hardening their hearts until they have lost not only their money but their souls. Some time ago a party of tourists traveling through Death Valley, California, discovered the skeleton of a man who had died on the drifting dunes of the desert. Clutched in his bony hand was a chunk of mica whose pyrites, resembling gold, had deceived him. He had mistaken the yellow streaks in this rock for gold. On a scrap of paper under the skeleton were written the words, "Died rich." He had thought he was rich, but starved to death, lost and alone. Such is the deceitfulness of riches. If we have nothing more than money, we are poor indeed.

There are many people who think they are rich in economic security, but they are actually poor toward God. One of the saddest pictures in the New Testament is that of the rich young ruler leaving Jesus sorrowfully, with his pockets full but his heart empty. He was interested in eternal life, but he wasn't willing to pay the price. That is true in the lives of many today. Many, like this rich youth, know the way — but they are not willing to pay the price.

It is not a sin to be rich. If you have gotten your riches honestly, then God considers you a steward of that which He has given you. But if your riches have choked out your spiritual life, then it has become sin—and you are poverty-

stricken in God's sight. We read about a number
of rich men in the Bible who were righteous and
godly men, who dedicated their riches to God.

In comparison to the rest of the world, almost
every American is considered a rich person. If
you have shoes to wear, clothes on your back
and food to eat, by the world's standards you
are rich. So the sin of avarice is actually one
of the great sins, and probably the greatest
stumbling block to the kingdom of heaven in
America today.

There are many people who say that the sin
of avarice is incurable and that once a man is
being choked by this sin that there is no salvation. I grant you that Jesus warned that it
is easier for a camel to go through the eye of a
needle than it is for a man who trusts in riches
to get to heaven (Matthew 19:24); yet it is
possible for a person who is guilty of this sin
to be saved. You may be actually a poor person, but greed and lust for money have hardened
your heart and made you bitter and envious.
It is possible for even you to be saved. You may

come in repentance of your sin and faith in the Lord Jesus Christ, and His blood can cleanse from every sin. You can find wonderful, glorious and blessed forgiveness at the foot of the Cross — no matter what your sin.